The Blue Rock Collection

FORREST GANDER is the author of five poetry books, including *Science & Steepleflower* and *Torn Awake* (both from New Directions). His most recent books of translation include *No shelter: Selected Poems by Pura López Colomé* and (with Kent Johnson) *Immanent Visitor: Selected Poems of Jaime Saenz*. His essays have appeared widely in such journals as *The Nation* and *The Boston Review*. With degrees in geology and English, he is Director of the Graduate Program in Literary Arts and Professor of Comparative Literature at Brown University.

RIKKI DUCORNET is the author of two short-story collections, five books of poetry, and seven novels, including *The Fan-Maker's Inquisition* and *Gazelle*. She is also a painter whose work has been exhibited widely. She lives in Denver, Colorado.

The Blue Rock Collection

FORREST GANDER

Artwork by Rikki Ducornet

SALT

CAMBRIDGE

PUBLISHED BY SALT PUBLISHING
PO Box 937, Great Wilbraham, Cambridge PDO CB1 5JX United Kingdom
PO Box 202, Applecross, Western Australia 6153

First published 2004
Reprinted 2005

Printed and bound in the United Kingdom by Lightning Source

Typeset in Swift 9.5 / 13

ISBN 1 84471 045 9 paperback

SP

1 3 5 7 9 8 6 4 2

For Christopher Dewdney for his Spring Trances,
Brenda Hillman for her Cascadia, *and*
Craig Dworkin for his "Tectonic Grammar"

Contents

Acknowledgments

"Pastoral" was first published in *The Kenyon Review*. "Field Guide to Southern Virginia" was first published in *Sulfur*. It was reprinted in *Science & Steeple-flower* (New Directions, 1997). "The Blue Rock Collection" was first published in *Ironwood*. It was reprinted in *Lynchburg* (University of Pittsburgh Press, 1993). "Line of Descent" was first published in *Conjunctions*. It was reprinted in *Torn Awake* (New Directions, 2001). Drawings by Rikki Ducornet were made expressly for this book and have not been published previously. "A Poetic Essay on Creation, Evolution and Imagination" was first published, in variant forms, in *Poets & Writers* magazine, and subsequently in *Faithful Existence* (Shoemaker and Hoard).

The author would like to thank the Geology Department at The College of William and Mary.

Pastoral

Prime pry prime me rocks prime evil rocks form
road's prime road's steep pry rocks form or pry
from rocks for eve the steep prime ore the road's
border rocks form prime the road's steep or all

Much have much they have there they have fir or
and faced there bore and door story have they
faced much first and much and last have they first faced
story of the trans the much in the trans long or it of
earth's long earth's of in long or door of the trans it
in door or of it order of the trans the story in or

What they but what in cast they cord what cull in
cast and but they cull cord in recast what colour
cord but cast and what cast ore record they in
is that two passed we that we that two passed is
two is that two is passed is that that is that passed

Line of Descent

Against the backdark, bright

    riband flickers of heat lightning. Nearer

  hills begin to show, to come clear

      as a hard, detached

         and glimmering brim

    against light lifting there. And here, pitched over

the braided arroyo choked with debris,

     a tent, its wan, cakey,

  road-rut color. On the front stake, two

green dragonflies, riding each other, pause.

    Look! cries the boy, running, the father behind him

    running too —

     and the canyon opening

out in front of them its magisterial consequence, cramming

  vertiginous air down its throat—

       to *snatch him*

    from the scarp.

Having heard the man

bellow, dikes of igneous rock

intrude a sedimentary sequence.

Squirms from his grasp. At the adjoining

campsite, a dark-haired tourist

reorients his view south

to the bordering plateau. Turns

away, a quick cut in bedding

planes. *Should they meet*

at the water pump, he imagines, stepping

onto a thin-crusted slippery clump, the flood-

odor of mule dung, and the boy

looks up at him.

When one is well-defined, is the other

uncertain? When wind-smoothed sandstone,

a torn map. The boy

and man at 6 a.m.

and the Vishnu outcrop

at fifteen hundred million years. When one

is certain. Stops the father

heaving and empty. The sea

sloshed landward

from east to west

spilling fossils. Eyes closed,

he focuses

on a speck of pain, the speck

of *How-am-I-this-man?*

to keep it from floating away. To dig out

the dead part. Tiny red flowers

curl on long lashes beside their boots.

In and out of self-forgetfulness.

A gila woodpecker eyes them

from its hollow saguaro.

The normative allure of encounter. In

and out. Lowers

    his head in voiceless spirants

        as the boy, with a Swiss pocketknife,

whittles his pencil.

In Bright Angel Shale,

balled trilobites. An ant escapes

from the ant-lion and

Deus ex machina!—

the boy dangles it over

the ant-lion pit and drops it back in.

Who can peel back the observing

and climb into presence?

The man? He tries to give himself

to curiosity but is hauled back

into semblance's

desert where things of the world are

distorted. What he feels is distorted.

As though it were theater and he

were scripted no words and a terrible fear of—

And dropped, with a child, into a dry,

crumbly excavation.

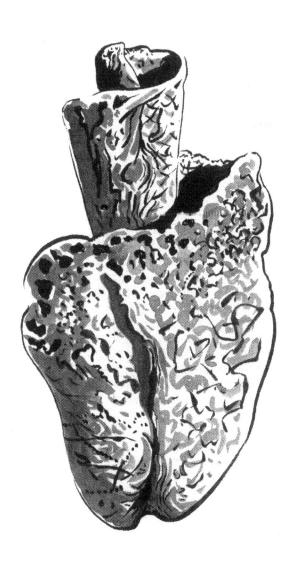

For want of time

                     insists the father the boy

undress by the sink

                     in the KOA washroom

inflexibly travertine

                     a crowded assembly of males

the boy angling in tears

                     at the top of an inner gorge

for the privacy of a stall

On varved clay,

    the boy hunches at an oozing

        gap in the record. Under his boot,

                pieces of Redwall

    break away

    and the fresh rock turns out

        to be grey. Crimson, finger shaped

bruises

    stripe his triceps.

Fifth hour of hike: vultures jod-

jod heads from the long ramping

boughs of a desert willow. At

this point in the father's story the boy

detests Odysseus

for betraying Philoctetes. Composite

revulsion built from

fragmentary telling.

The silts laid down. Swears,

I will not *grip his arms*

in anger again, the

man—

A clock we can use

to gauge term and event. A record

of transgressions. In the early

moon, the man wakes to bats—

fluttered-up from the same Cretacious stock

from which sprang Condylarths—and the boy

on his elbows *watching him*.

What is the preferred

orientation

of an early blue thrust fault? That is

grit in his mouth or is it

the immanent making

its announcement? When one is

well-defined—

The boy shears and rolls in dream

on the slippery sleeping bag

giving himself

an erection. And if each

image, each line

on the horizon yields

to another, when do the meanings of

perception dig in?

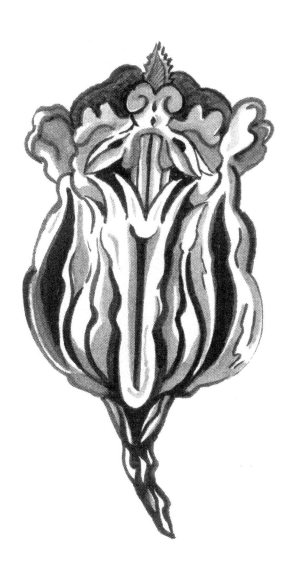

Canyon walls compress

  concordant shifts. Heat, and fossil

       footprints wink across

 the Supai. Battened to the trill of light,

violet skinks. Clack! the boy claps

  rock with rock. A barked

    reproach evaporates

from the sedimentary progression. Slowly.

  They walk slowly

    who descend into

      beginning, like animals led

  toward an altar, the one stumbling

      under a backpack, the one dawdling to catch

   horned toads.

A caustic tongue scorching into them.

An inward face of identity

                             mimics the strata.

       LOST, the stick-pierced paper says, but *what-*

                  was-lost has washed away. Come

         to the edge of language, he finds the edge

        is inside language. Coiled

            within him the monster

whose emotion is impatience whose tongue is hiss.

                         Aroused, the head

         rises and strikes. And yet, who would not

                crawl on his belly, mouth in dust,

      to know he had not ruined it? To learn

                a way out. At the stream, the boy asks

why his friends would leave Philoctetes

       alone on an island. He tugs off the boy's boot,

                  massaging his chafed tendon

           between thumb and forefinger.

The principle of original horizontality.

Dry heat, no sweat, empty canteens. A siesta

in late afternoon buff-light.

Fanning the sprawled boy

with a torn map

to keep off impetuous, clamoring flies.

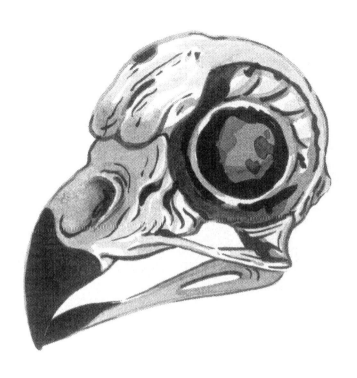

Two hours after the major
        unconformity, the canyon's rim
    eclipses the sun. Through Cambrian talus
                pit vipers unwind — true
        heirs to the pineal eye.
            A man recounts Greek plays to the boy
        phosphorescent with dust
    while wrens drop
        vertically through dwarf pines rooted
                in foliate schists
            chirping *seed*,

                seed.

The Blue Rock Collection

Igneous

GRANITE (SLAB)

They will slaughter you

pray for you and wish you peace

but there is something wrong with this.

GABBRO

Scarecrow

in the field

with a bow

and arrow.

LAVA

I wake on

the futon,

a stream

of ants shining

to the baseboard from

the cut in my palm.

MOON

moon

Metamorphic

HORNEBLENDE SCHIST

A deer in the sun
covered with flies.

OPHICALCITE MARBLE

Two tendons
     sieze the throat
pulleying
     her breasts taut.

SERPENTINE

Green came to the forest
like Helen Traubel's voice.

Crystals

GEODE

You are entitled to

              be uncertain:

        swallow the Cambrian

tongue, now crack

the head crammed with teeth.

TOURMALINE

The man who will not pay dues.

    The moonshine

in which a cottonmouth steeps.

YELLOW QUARTZ

Men cruising

    the park. Dogs

        barking.

    In the

    highrise,

        lights.

GARNET

Politicians squeeze hands.

    Pigeon eyes.

Sedimentary

SANDSTONE

Across the quiet

river, fog spins out

blanking the doorsteps of houses

from which fathers shout

for children

and crumble

and have only their tiredness to go on.

DIATOMACIOUS LIMESTONE

In the roofless auditorium

soldiers are sleeping

under helmets and long snows.

Terms

PITCHEBLENDE

Light's skill is its failing.

PYRITE

I bet you are judging this poem already.

EROSION

We wake, drunk.
The planetarium
    locks into place
under our hair; we take
the bus,
    neurons flicking out in pairs.

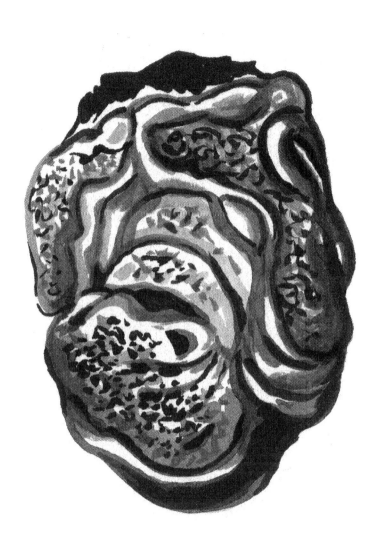

PLATE TECHTONICS

Tug   of slow war.

THE EARTH AS AN EVOLVED BODY

You enter the trap
        door, unlatch
the windows, open them.
                Grasshoppers are treadling
like women with thread. No one
is fond
            of burials here. At the root of each
                flower,
odor of baked bread.

Field Guide to Southern Virginia

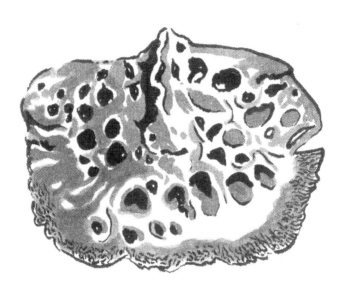

~

True as the circumference

to its center. Woodscreek Grocery,

Rockbridge County. Twin boys

peer from the front window, cheeks

bulging with fireballs. Sandplum trees

flower in clusters by the levee. She

makes a knot on the inside knob

and ties my arms up

against the door. Williamsburg green.

With a touch as faint as a watermark.

Tracing cephalon, pygidium, glabella.

~

Sway-back, through freshly cut stalks,

stalks the yellow cat. Can you smell

where analyses end, the orchard

oriole begins? Slap her breasts lightly

to see them quiver. Delighting in this.

Desiccation cracks and plant debris

throughout the interval. In the Black-

water River, fishnets float

from a tupelo's spongy root

chopped into corks. There may be sprawling

precursors, descendent clades there are none.

~

The gambit declined was less

promising. So the flock of crows

slaughtered all sixty lambs. Toward the east, red

and yellow colors prevail.

Praying at the graveside,

holding forth the palm of his hand

as a symbol of God's book.

For the entirety of the Ordovician.

With termites, Mrs. Elsinore explained,

as with the afterlife, remember:

there are two sides to the floor. A verb

for inserting and retrieving

green olives with the tongue. From

the scissure of your thighs.

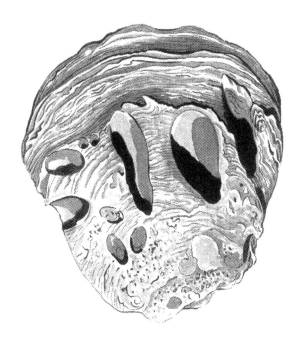

~

In addition, the trilobites

were tectonically deformed. Snap-on

tools glinting from magenta

loosestrife, the air sultry

with creosote and cicadas.

You made me to lie down in a peri-Gondwanan back-arc basin.

Roses of wave ripples and gutter casts.

Your sex hidden by goat's beard.

Laminations in the sediment. All

preserved as internal molds

in a soft lilac shale.

~

Egrets picketing the spines of cattle in fields edged

with common tansy. Flowers my father gathered

for my mother to chew. To induce abortion. A common,

cosmopolitan agnostoid lithofacies naked in the foothills. I love

the character of your intelligence, its cast as well as pitch.

Border wide without marginal spines. At high angles

to the inferred shoreline.

~

It is the thin flute of the clavicles, each rain-pit

above them. The hypothesis of flexural loading. Aureoles

pink as steepleflower. One particular day, four hundred

million years ago, the mud stiffened

and held the stroke of waves. Orbital motion.

Raking leaves from the raspberries, you

uncover a nest of spring salamanders.

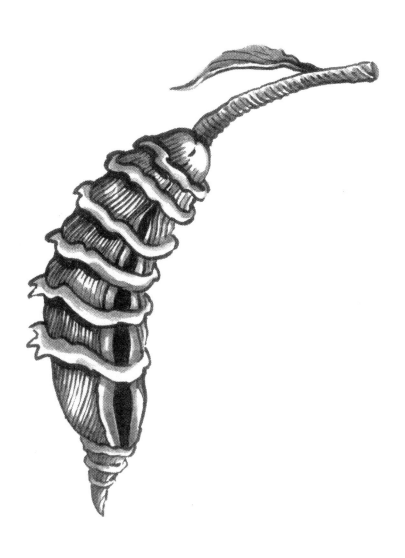

Facing in All Directions

Resting on her belly, her long-fingered hands suggest she is

    pregnant. It might be

September, when the full-bore orchestration of insects rusts out,

    goes tinny.

By the way he has raised his hand to her face

as though it were an innovation on faces or merely the envelope

for his admiring, as though a hand could say *thou, we recognize*

    them,

lovers who have rushed

             to the wood's edge

on trails of inference

through all the thicknesses of scattered and divergent signs,

flying the contagion. What plague this time? What time?

As if there were a safe house, some renunciation to grope toward. Look:

he is still a boy even, an eagerness

                   he has let her pare

into the avowal that unlocked her eyes. And if

in his pocket he carries a flute carved

from the hollow ulna of a red-crowned crane,

and if in her kiss he can taste black pills she has swallowed to

    stop

the bleeding, it is not in the brief conspectus of

                        their history according to Durer

who shows us, us alone, the skeleton behind them

unleaning from a tree

as a tense might be unbound. The couple pause

to appraise each other, their miraculous escape

                              from a fatality

that leads precisely here. As it always does.

But warning birds have yet to fly up in their faces. Briefly,

however briefly, they outstrip ordination.

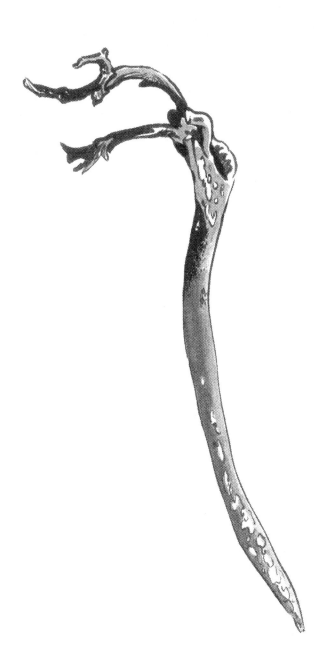

～

Then the sun's limb darkens, clouds roll in, and when rains let up

no one is there. Only two stalk-eyed flies fighting on a stump. In a

distant city

once named for the white thighs of its women, pigeons

blister Sacre Coeur's dome. Dim, early morning, on Blvd. St. Germain,

phalanxes of sycamore thicken with seed balls. Raiding

the palace, a grimy throng rouses the queen from sleep.

As hallways swell with shouting, she gathers herself

into her gown

and stumbles to the ante-room

known as the Oeil-de-Boeuf. Although she rehearsed

these moments, each gesture is fraught, each effort invested

in others, an architecture of ornament she cannot begin to put together.

What a quivering in the walls as the great doors bow inward. Like candles

on a sumptuous table,

the evenly-spaced steps of her fleeing,

the little coils of scent swirling up from each footprint

conspire to weigh her down. And while she pounds at the king's

chamber,

a single bellow

fills the hall of mirrors, as though a huge mouth were coming

to swallow the remaining ripe hours

already dished for her to try.

Always: as though a huge mouth were coming.

But days warm and the tourists walk on

through the palace, through an incessant storm of cometary grains,

swayed by plans for lunch,

by rear-guard obligations. One shopping cart

rammed into another. Little failures leading to blankness.

The Seine rises and oceans rise and from their lightless floors,

giant worms,

mouthless

and gutless, wave.

~

                    Dear C, do you remember finding

this rock in the garden? Grey-blue silicious slate. It burrowed up

through the million years of sedimentary facies

between begotten

          and born. Events

occur as discourse, it's true, but who

would read the stone or say at such-and-such a point, at these

          coordinates of

                              August luster

and the ratcheting of cicadas, it entered the drama

                    interrupting life as it was lived and known.

It brought no plague; it has no mouth, a word

I write and see your mouth, the star

in your lower lip where once your tooth went through.

No warning birds. No slackening of the river.

~

An alluvial scar incised
by a river is like the gnash of arriving through thought at words.
   And words
themselves can be compared to stones,
relentless systems of reference. On the island of Cyprus, amid
      rubble
from the earthquake that obliterated Kourion
                        in 365 A.D., they found
the skeletons of a young man,
a woman, and their eighteen month old child.
The man's arm circled the woman's waist, his left leg,
                        as though to shield her,
he had thrown across her pelvis. He held her hand and clutched
      the child.
Bliss comes uncounting the hour, seizing no set moment. Some
claim there isn't time to consider the whole of the story or
the interdependence of its characters. Some say every meaning
      will be revealed
until the last witness is lost and gone.

Coda: About the Second Circle

Don't expect relief anytime soon,

I heard a voice snicker.

His name was Coffin who called me to his mouth,

saying Whose bier was hauled in a black Cadillac? Yours.

Whose body glowed orange-red? Yours.

Whose incandescent enthusiasm—almost transparent—

gradually thickened to a dark, dull red

barely perceptible in daylight? Do not forget,

your buttocks belong to me.

He was a baboon-headed god holding an ibis.

One thing I learned was not to argue,

but when he handed me the eye

that was lacking from his head, I

threw it, instinctively, into the fire.

Now they all tell me I should have known better.

Crystallizing into diamond and heliotrope and agate,

it hissed like scale from a hot piece of iron

hammered on the blacksmith's anvil.

When I looked up he was wielding a cow-mouthed chisel

and a four pound cross-pein hammer.

I am he to whom an amulet is attached every night.

It is true, I admit, that certain men's sweat

is endowed with a certain savor.

A Poetic Essay
on Creation, Evolution,
and Imagination

I.

With CD Wright, I co-edit a literary book press,

    Lost Roads Publishers. Lost Roads, because the map,

  as poet Jack Spicer reminds us, is not

      the territory. Like an anthropologist, an editor

might look for the missing link, the lost species,

    to understand the picture, which is

      a picture in time. I am interested

     in evolution and in the proliferation

of poetries. I know that only

    the collective assemblage of fossils,

      of enunciations, can establish

    the character of a system. We

readily find Derek Walcott's poetry, but

  when we discover the apposing

    poetics of fellow islanders

      Kamau Brathwaite and Shake Keane, our scope

  widens and the meanings of Walcott's work

    change too. Poetry

doesn't compete, Louis Zukofsky

  asserted; it is added to like science.

Like species, poems are not invented, but

develop out of a kind of discourse, each

poet tensed

against another's poetics, in conversation,

like casts of wormtrails

in a sandstone. Our mineral attention

can fill in the imprint, memorializing it. But each

discovery we make

only alludes to the diversity, the breadth

of the unrecorded, the un-championed. When

are your poetics,

your politics,

not implicated in another's?

History reminds us that any scientific truth is a

construct

and a contract with its time.

At the time when Aristotle and

Theophrastus were starting a university in Greece, it was

commonly assumed that stones

like limonite nodules — which often have detached cores

rattling around inside them—

were pregnant. In one of the first treatises

on the science of geology, Theophrastus

asserted that lyngurium, what we now call

tourmaline, a gem carved by ancient Greek jewelers

into signets, is a precipitate

of lynx urine. A wild lynx,

in fact, produced better stones than a tame one. Nevertheless,

Theophrastus commented, only experienced

searchers can find lyngurium. Why?

Because after a lynx passes its urine,

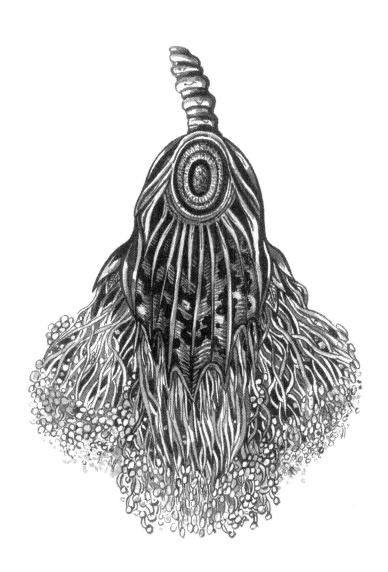

it conceals it, scraping dirt

over the liquid which, buried now, begins

to harden into stone.

But Theophrastus's conjecture — that animals

might generate or harbor stones — is not

farfetched. Contemporary scientists tell us that

lodged within the bodies of various

organisms, from homing pigeons to whales, a mineral of

iron and oxygen, magnetite,

serves as a kind of internal compass, helping them

to sense the earth's magnetic field

and so

to navigate. A crayfish

requires a grain of sand lodged in its "ear"

(at the base of its antennule) before it can

balance underwater. Chickens,

of course, swallow pebbles for digestion. And mammals

disgorge hairballs which can be mineral-hard. In fact,

one impressive bezoar-stone, a fist-sized fossil hairball,
presides over the living room table of poet Clayton Eshleman.

In the thirteenth century, Albertus Magnus
        detailed the methods for softening gems
                with goat's blood, urine, and milk.
                    To temper steel, he recommended that
            the metal be heated
        white-hot and plunged repeatedly
                into a liquid rendered from radish juice and
                    fluid from crushed earthworms.

With Socrates' assurance guiding
            his sight, Da Vinci put aside his dissecting knife
    and noted, wrongly, that
            a man's liver has five lobes.

What Theophrastus, Albertus Magnus, and

Da Vinci saw corroborated *what they thought they would see*

according to the prevalent assumptions of their times.

But neither good poetry nor

good science corroborates

the assumption of presumed values.

Because habits of thought often determine

presumptions, it can be worthwhile to keep a watch out

every which-way for the real thing. Electronic

poems, slams, computer-generated sequences,

translations: energy

flows into new forms.

If you want to find the second-hottest body

in the solar system, don't assume it will be found

next to the hottest, the sun. Io,

one of Jupiter's moons,

kneaded between the gravitational

forces of Jupiter and Europa

into an ultramafic magma

the consistency of olive oil, spews

lava as hot as 3,100 degrees.

How readily reality

adapts to the imagination! Physicist Richard

Feynman, known especially for his work

with uncertainty, suggested that antiparticles

might be ordinary particles traveling backward

in time. His insight was elicited

not by daunting mathematics but

by his curiously simple-looking arrow diagrams,

which suddenly made the idea seem plausible.

The diagrams themselves

conceived an intuition, the scribble

suggests a word. Sometimes an organ

precedes its function. A structure arises, but

becomes useful only after

its development. Evolutionary theorists call this

exaptation. Our brains may have

developed this way. The human is

the animal

who lays-in meaning. The poem is

a structure in which meanings resonate.

There is another world, the poet Paul Eluard

famously wrote, *but it is inside*

this one. And quite literally so. Certain

bacteria live hundreds of meters

within the earth's crust, taking nourishment

from dissolved gases and minerals

that form through the reaction

of groundwater and rock. These bacteria,

chemolithotrophs, have no need

for solar energy. Some scientists

estimate that the underground biomass,

the world inside this one,

might be more than double

the living mass at the surface of our

planet.

Perhaps we can understand now

what the 19th-century German naturalist, Alexander

von Humboldt meant when

he spoke of "the all animatedness of the earth."

In his own time, Giovanni Battista

Vico argued against clear, distinct,

Cartesian ideas, emphasizing instead

practical wisdom and *ingenium*, the power

of connecting separate and diverse elements.

It is his path that interests me.

On another path,

exhausted after searching for

traces of hominids in Northern Tanzania, Mary

Leakey's crew began clowning around,

throwing elephant dung

at each other. Ducking, one young

man's face brushed ground that had been covered —

three and a half million years before — with a

carbonitite-rich

volcanic ash. Rains

had turned the ash into cement. There,

just under his nose, he discovered

the most significant Paleolithic path, the Laetoli

footprints

which show that early hominids

were fully bipedal long before

they developed tool-making capabilities or

an expanded brain. Twenty-seven

meters of tracks left by two males, a female,

and a hipparion. Poet

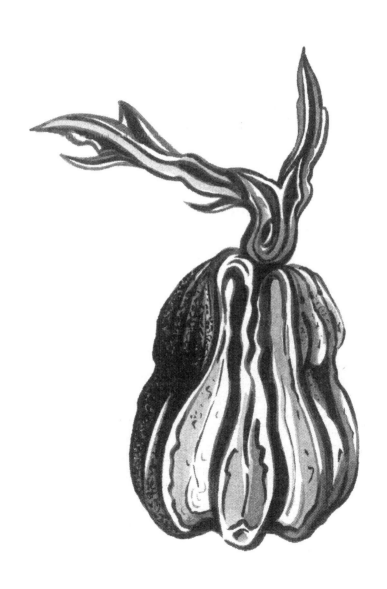

Gary Snyder urges us to find our own

way, *off the road, on the path.*

Wrote Wittgenstein, "We feel

that even if all possible scientific questions

be answered, the problems of life

have not been touched at all."

At one time, scientific method meant

that we chopped something apart

and put it back together; we made

a machine. That method

has endured as a scientific model, and

a very successful one, for it

predicts that when we do something, we

will obtain certain results.

But such

methodology is not a universal, embracing

all human experience. If we approach

with a different model, we will ask

different questions.

Is it Whitman who suggests that

in the beauty of poems we will find

"the tuft and final applause of science"? Metaphor

argues against logic.

The forest, say the Pygmies,

gives us everything we need — food, clothing,

shelter, warmth... and affection.

In order to more fully understand death,

Dr. Cabinas applied himself

scientifically. Over several years,

he recorded detailed studies of the movements

of decapitated bodies

just after execution. What was it

that he learned?

Until three hundred million

years ago, fish were strictly bottom feeders

within the water column. Insect wings,

like those of the green nymph stick insect

pinned to the wall above my desk,

evolved

from the moveable, articulated gill plates

of ancient, aquatic insects

escaping those fish. Writing

is like evolution in that poems

are not invented so much as they develop

in the act of writing. Robert Creeley:

I see as I write.

And evolution

is contingent in nature. We are here

by chance. John Ashbery: *It could always have been*

written differently. Or, as the poet Basil Bunting

put it succinctly:

Man is not end product, maggot asserts.

We must force ourselves open

to discoveries across the grain, contrary

to what we "know."

In this, we may be led

best by silence, an almost

religious gesture of openness

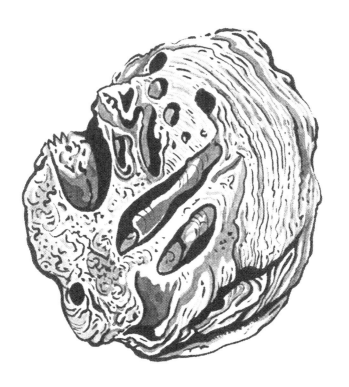

II.

It is said that the powers of a Noh actor

can be assessed simply on

the basis of his *kamae*, an immobile position

giving the impression of unshakeable balance

and intense presence. His muscles are not tight, but

neither are they relaxed. Consciousness is focused

on all parts of the body simultaneously. *Kamae*

is a posture open to all eventualities,

virtual movement.

In the Noh play *Sekedira Komachi*, reputed

to be the most difficult of all

to perform, the *shite* or main actor

must sit completely motionless, masked,

at the front of the stage for an hour and a half,

expressing corporeal intensity by his very restraint of movement.

Art is not the waging of taste only

nor the exercise of argument,

but like love the experience of vision, the revelation of—.

Perhaps eros is the fundamental condition of that

escalation of meaning necessary to poetry, and of

cognition itself. The father of Western logic,

Socrates, claimed that he had only one real talent:

to recognize at once

the lover and the beloved.

In those very years when Socrates

was making himself the gadfly of Athens, the Maya

in Central America were building an extensive civilization.

According to their beliefs, the world had already ended

several times. It had come to an end once by fire,

once by water. The final apocalypse, the one they predicted for

our time,

would be brought about by . . . hubbub, commotion.

Maybe the so-called contemporary indifference

to poetry is nothing more than dread,

dread that poetry is so penetrated by silence.

Because I am not silent the poems are bad.

George Oppen.

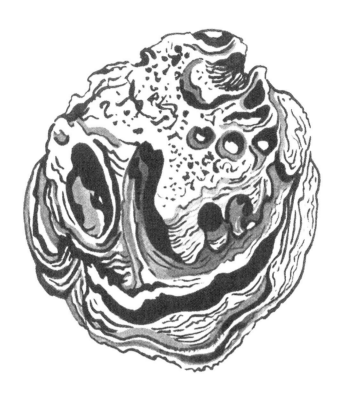

Since some genes mutate

at regular rates, the average number of genetic differences

between species in two orders serves as a clock,

showing when these animals shared a common

ancestor. The common mammalian ancestor

can be dated, in this way, to one hundred million years ago. This

is about twenty million years before

the first appearance of mammals in the fossil record.

Lost roads

underlie the known roads. Lost roads

and silence.

And isn't memory itself a crumpled map
of lost roads crisscrossing body and brain? We
are not surprised to learn that there are several
memory systems: *semantic* (long-term memory for concepts),
episodic (long-term memory for events), *short-term*, and
implicit, or unconscious memory. Experiences of our past
are constructed by combining
bits of information
from several levels of knowledge.

And we know emotional and physical states
strongly influence what is remembered. And
our endocrinal system is clearly involved
in our thinking. Wrote poet Paul Valery:
At the end of the mind the body; but
at the end of the body, the mind.

Unlike lyrical language, with which

we were gifted, the language of science has been

agreed upon. In a poem, the terms are unique,

irreplaceable; they can only be quoted. But the terms

for scientific language are written across

an equal sign; science is predominately expressed

as a language of equivalences, of substitutions. Poetry

is perhaps the ultimate challenge

to any language of substitution

as well as to

the newspaper's language of managed reality. For me,

it is the discourse

in which the greatest energy

is still possible.

Once, the language of science was thought

to be characterized by precision and the absence

of ambiguity. Faith in the potential of a literal language

bolstered assumptions of picture theories of meaning, what

Bertrand Russell and Ludvig Wittgenstein

were working on together, and these

theories reached their peak in the doctrine of logical

positivism, the notion that reality

might be described through language

in a testable way.

But cognition, as both Coleridge and

Keats suggested, savoring

negative capability, is only

the result of mental construction. Nobel physicist

Richard Feynman believed

in the primacy of doubt

as the essence of knowing.

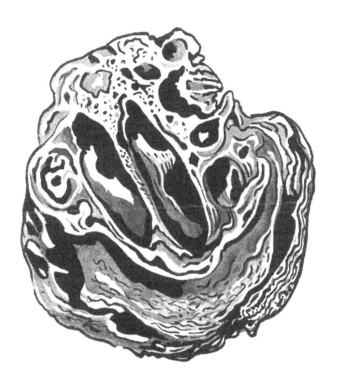

The objective world is not
directly accessible but is constructed
on the basis of constraints on our perception and
on our language. Language,
perception,
and memory are inextricably
interdependent. There is no one real world
toward which science proceeds
by successive approximations. As the poet William Bronk
wrote: *And oh, it is always a world
and not the world.* There is no neutral,
objective point of view.

III.

Look where the field of dickcissels is

    swirling up into a tornado of wings. Now
look down —

    and you might see the swirl of mud

    created on the bottom of a pond

        by the withdrawal of an alligator snapping turtle's
head. A species traceable

        to the early Miocene, the alligator snapper
is the largest freshwater turtle. In 1937,

    Hall and Smith cited a specimen

            weighing 403 pounds caught in the Neosho River

        in Cherokee City, Kansas. When it would strike,
    its entire upper body lifted off the ground

            as it lunged forward like a Volkswagen.

Human muscle is packed with strands
called mitochondria which create
heat in all warm-blooded animals. But
mitochondria cannot contract. For this reason,
reptiles, which are cold-blooded,
have muscles much stronger
than mammals.

I have raised from a hatchling
a baby alligator snapper. But
for the egg tooth and its small size,
the young turtle resembles
perfectly the adult. It has a reduced shell
with a very small, cross-shaped
plastron exposing its underparts. Its head
is large, the jaws extremely strong, and

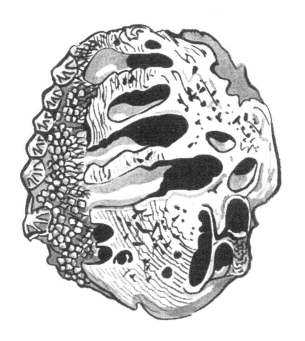

the upper beak is hooked. There are

    paired barbels on the chin and

        several irregularly shaped lamina

at the under-edges of the shell. The tail

    is long, armed above

        with erect bony scales. Snapping turtles

have been known to bite

    the snouts of horses

as they attempted to drink. They are the only

  animals ever observed

    to share holes, unmolested,

with a bull alligator.

The primitive alligator snapping turtle,

little removed from the lost

road of the dinosaurs, represents

a transitional group in vertebrate

evolution, between aquatic fishes

and terrestrial birds and mammals. As it lies

underwater, it slowly opens

and closes its mouth as its throat pulsates. If

we added dye to the water

in the tank, it would confirm

swirling currents near its mouth.

The throat-pulsing

increases with the length of the turtle's

submersion, until the animal begins

gulping water. There has been

some speculation that the alligator

snapping turtle, *Macroclemys temmincki*,

is capable of pharyngeal respiration. Most

of the time, it lies

mutely below the surface of the water

like a cloistered monk, looking up. Because

it is omnivorous, because it is open

to anything

and everything, all roads

lead to its mouth. It waits,

listening, in silence.

Perhaps this is the most basic gesture

of the poet.

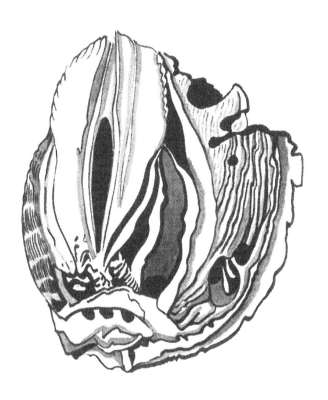

Burning Towers, Standing Wall

"In a ceremony filled with pride and painful memories,
New York officials laid a 20-ton slab of granite yesterday
as the cornerstone of a new tower . . ."
—*LA Times*, JULY 5, 2004

I.

At sunset the surface of the wall gleams gold gleaming

and seems from even a short distance a smooth

impenetrable force swelling forward to meet the light

or the gaze of the visitor to the Maya ruin and locals

offer their service as guides or show what they mean

to sell in a mixed language of numbers and night

disperses everyone but the insects crawling into fissures

in the crumble, field stones and mortar and flat

stacking stones, which divide what from what once

So doves come, a spotted turkey, iguana and

lately a pair of trogons to sit like lords on the ruin

where rocks flake away in rain and birdshit

in which seeds set, shell-stripped in the digestive tracks

of the birds or wind-sown,

sending up stem and aigrette into unkind light

and wind, while colorless thread thin roots

force cracks in the capstones to give way, rain and sunbake

dissolving mafic bonds as the exposure spreads

inward

Some of the sounds bouncing from the stones are

nearly the same sounds, resonant, human

voices and the *perwicka perwicka*

of a quetzal in flight at a distance

and they almost give us access

through the grind of cicada wings and

crickets thrumming serrated thighs,

although the high rubato laugh of children

or a woman's voice rising at the end of a phrase, her eyes

locked on her infant's eyes as she walked close to the wall,

those domestic acoustics

have precipitated out, leaving

a gravitas around the ruin and into this

the walls swell with oxidation

and orange lichens press outward, the stones flake

away from their interior registry of rain

and termite clatter and the chimuck of falling pebbles, sounds

stones draw inward along

the cleavage planes of their minerals so that

if decibels diminish

as they approach impossible silence

but never entirely fade out,

this fresh patter is stirred into a vibrating, immeasurably

thin memorial ache inside the walls

and as primordial

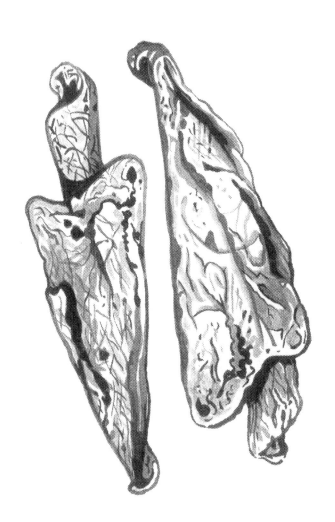

II.

What came over the walls was drought, the 206 year

cyclical brightening of the sun, umber dust from the fields lifted

and blew into joints between stones, the pocks in the stones,

boys running along the god-faced wall

wiped their fingers on an altar

freshly carved from soft green

trachyte already hardening, exposed to air,

into a delicate grey,

fewer and fewer hand marks,

the number of shadows across the stones dwindling,

the same number of walls, resilient limestone blocks quarried

with quartz and wood tools, bound together

with mud-gravel and zahcab, a lime cement

mixed in small batches, plastered on the stones with ceiba

trowels and fingers, the occasional crisp imprints of fir needles

from a thousand years ago visible

still in the desiccated mortar

What came over the walls was the enemy the conquered ones

the immiserated poor the infidels who

scaled stones on the knotted rope of their alien language

on spikes of vengeance with fire this section of the wall

shivered then and this part split open, thatch and wooden lintels

burned as the enemy climbed through

the pitch and rhythm of their shouting rebounded from the stones

and fading screams clotted-off in smoke that veiled the city and

licked into those meticulous slits that represent

the iris of the human eye in figures

stuccoed to the temple's collapsing roof

What came over the wall was disease a plague

the priests could not avert a plague that made the stone

builders distrust each other and steal away

from walls they laid in a square clearing on the dark

scarp of a mountain and plague followed them

into the wilderness with a yowl like a clay saucer

making circles on the floor,

and though, as ever, cumulonimbus

pompadoured over the far mountains,

crows swirled above

the abandoned pyramid and king vultures

drove them off and even sea birds flew in and

squawked from the walls in hordes

ransacking corpses for their flesh and the stones

were white-crested and dribbled argent bird-lime

The Spaniards blew up the walls to see

behind them blasted the walls and crushed them

to pave roads to extinguish the trace the refuge

of the heathen to make noise they

mutilated stelae rubbed out the glyphs the bark

codices burned and the temple frieze behind the stelae,

and to the traces of blood and resin in braziers and on

altar stones they sluiced fresh blood, they chipped away

a relief carving in pumice of the former

ruler holding a manikin scepter, the facing stones

squared, well-smoothed and fitted

toppled into a monolithic mass of rubble and

mortar no girder still itself among

What lifts over the wall are gnats, iridescent butterflies,

a haze of mosquitoes, the night carousing

click-songs of wukus or cacomixtles

rummaging through the showy blossoms

of a Capparis tree whose trunk and roots

hold back the rubbish of the wall where it breached,

something that leaves the relicts of katydids in its feces

comes over the wall,

and the scent of nectar comes over the wall,

the anniversaries of eyes.

III.

One over two, two over one. You must look
until you find the flat side of a round stone.
Don't put the largest on the bottom, but assemble
a communion. They rise to the surface of fields
in the rainy season.

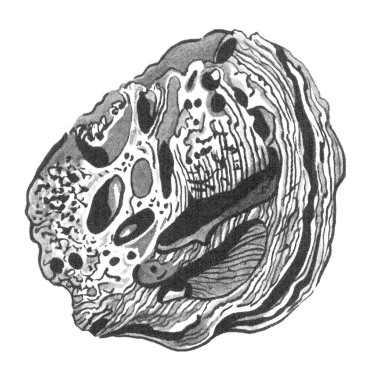

One over two, two over one. Shim the round
stone with the flat. Lay a cross-stone here
to bind thicknesses. After you harvest
sandstone, use a chert wedge to bevel a fissure
where you want it to break. One
over two, stagger the joints.

Two over one, one over two. This stone weighs

three arrobas and no man could lift it. We are given

to understand that by means of a special whistle

the stones, large as they are,

arranged themselves

without any help to form these walls

for the first upright people.

Position the flatter side upward. Mix the crushed and burnt limestone in a calcite bowl to render sticky plaster. Start at the bottom, work across, and then move up a row. Larger cap stones stabilize the walls. One over two, two over one.

An index finger dressing a joint will
fix in the mortar its print, an intimacy
to surpass every other gesture the hand
might have made. What went on
behind these walls and who stood here
and hissed out or was massacred
so that our imagination of them is saturated
with encounter? And what does it weigh down
if not the intuition of our relation,
a resonance? They who also heard
an echo of hammers and dogs upwelling
into their hills. And followed Venus with their eyes
on its transverse. And stood near this same wall
noting the caliber and flow of a stream of urine.
Two stones butted together in a course and another
stone laid over the seam. Who sopped-in
laughter and met pain with breath. And sank under
the ceaselessly breaking wave of event, *is*
conjugating *here*. The fragility of presence. A bird
perched at the tip of a branch. Singing, we say.